WHAT is past
is prologue. . .

(THE TEMPEST Act II)
William Shakespeare

MAY-MURDOCK PUBLICATIONS
Box 343/90 Glenwood Ave.,
Ross, CA 94957

UNTIL DEATH AND AFTER

HOW TO LIVE WITH A DYING INTIMATE

ACKNOWLEDGMENTS

PAGE 63

To my Mother

Marian Murdock Rattray

who in her final illness, after 82
years of active living, declared
with conviction and wonder, "Dying
is the experience of a lifetime."

Her 'good death' was a victory
to all concerned and removed for
us life's greatest fear - the fear of
our own mortality. . .

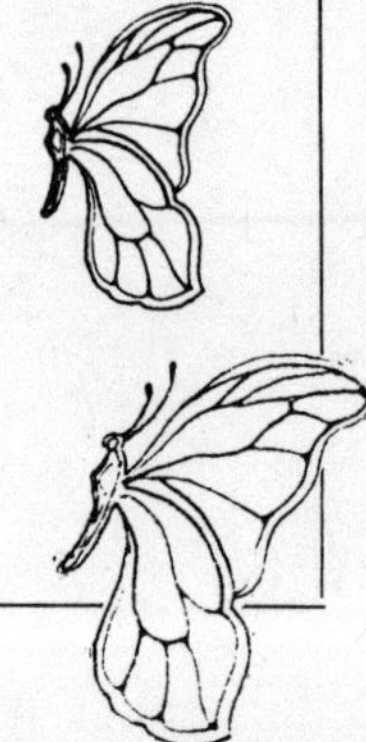

. . . And To My Husband

Dick Murdock

whose enthusiasm, praise, editor-
ship and perserverance at the IBM
Executive typewriter made this book
a reality.
It would have been impossible
without him.

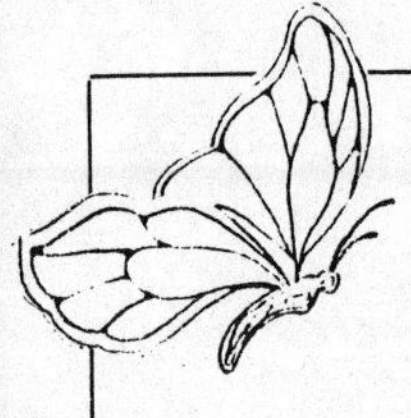

PREFACE

HOW DID YOU do it?" a friend with a dying father asked. "How did you care for your mother, handle the life of your family AND take care of yourself?"

I had no easy answer. There had been Hospice of Marin and the supportive involvement of my husband, children and sisters so I was never alone in the care.

However, I wanted to tell Cindy more, to have specific concrete suggestions. To that end, I asked friends met at hospice bereavement meetings over the past three years to answer for me, from their experiences, Cindy's questions: How did you do it? What helped you most? What can you tell my young friend?

Their answers, as different as their individual stories, also had amazing similarities which I've woven into this little book. Here, expanded and extended through the opinions of experts plus the intimacy of my own experiences, are words of help, hope and hospice.

Jayne Murdock

TOTAL loving care
is needed at
the end of life
just as it was
in the beginning. . .

E.K–R

Until Death...

DEATH - as a word, a fact - is something most of us tend to skirt, as though not saying the word will make the fact stay away. Or, conversely, as if speaking of death might be to court it. Dying happens to other people at other times in other places, not to us, not here, not now.

Yet suddenly, the reality of these words has been forced upon you. Not long ago you were told that someone you love has cancer (or another deteriorating terminal illness). Angry, shocked, frightened, heartbroken, you've cried and shouted, prayed and hoped. And you've gone on, stunned, with the business of daily living. You've since experienced the ups and downs of treatment and operations and their devastating effect upon that special person.

Now both face the last stages of dying, one the principal combatant, you an active participant. Treatment and recovery are no longer uppermost goals. Help for the patient, and you - the caregiver - consists at this point, of whatever measures best fortify morale, no simple task in the face of your disintegrating world.

What can you do when cure is out of the question, when death has changed from a nebulous word to a concrete fact?

FOR THE FIRST time there are choices, options open to those in your position, alternative measures, different modes of care.

Just as there are many who choose the adventure and closeness of home birth, a growing number are deciding to die at home rather than in the sterile unnatural atmosphere of most hospitals. More and more families like you, therefore, are dealing with dying on a very personal day-by-day basis. Involvement in home dying is not an easy choice. It carries with it deeper feelings than many of us have ever before faced. Rewards, however hard to believe now, are great for all concerned; the patient, you, the whole family, even the youngest. Children need to be honestly involved soon as possible when a family member is dying, and this is much easier to do at home.

THE TIME TO prepare a child for the trauma of another person's death is - as for all of us - long before the event itself," said George W. Williams[1], author of DEATH AND THE CHILD.

A child creates his own answer to situations if none is offered and that answer is often terrifying and bizarre. Children take words seriously and literally so it's important to use the right precise word, considering the child's cognitive level.

Once in doing word associations with my class, I discovered that a 7-year-old boy thought if his father were 'fired' he'd be thrown into a furnace where he worked. No wonder the tenuous employment situation in the family caused him bad dreams! Think for a moment of words a child can overhear and misunderstand when a family member is seriously ill and facing death.

1 - see page 62

Simple answers and honest explanations, geared to age, need to be lovingly given as questions arise, and even before. Your attitude does much to remove the fearful awesome mystery of sensing, but not understanding, that something untoward is happening.

Including children in the situation, at whatever level they can handle, helps everyone.

"Care for the dying," writes Avery D. Weisman,[2] professor of psychiatry at Massachusetts General Hospital and author of ON DYING AND DENYING, "should be seen as a privilege, not a duty imposed by guilt."

UNTIL DEATH - AND AFTER could instead be titled CARING FOR THE CAREGIVER. It's directed to you. You're in the midst of a difficult draining experience with so many demands - physically and emotionally - that at times you'll feel unable to make it through another night, another hour, another second.

But here, garnered from conversations, letters and reports of survivors, from books and articles by experts, plus personal experience with my mother's dying, are things proven helpful to us that may aid you.

Death and dying has been romanticized, simplified, lately. It is not always (or even often) like LOVE STORY. Nor is it usually as peaceful, right and beautiful as with my mother after 82 full years of living, supported and surrounded by a large loving family and the dedicated pain-control care of a hospice group. That was, if there is such a thing, a 'perfect dying.' Sometimes it's messy and ugly. Sometimes it's lonely and frightening. Sometimes it's cosmic outrage. ("Why this child, so innocent and vulnerable? Why this strong young man who has just begun to live? Why this mother with her tiny children? Why?")

Yet this outrage has to be met, this anger acknowl-

2 - see page 62

edged and expressed, this untimely unseemly death
faced and ultimately accepted. Not easy, it is perhaps
the most difficult emotional challenge in life.

Dr. Weisman talks of the essentials of a 'good
death' which he lists as care, choice, communication,
continuity, composure and closure. "Stripped of the
traditional terror and fears that cluster around
thoughts of death," he writes, "there are certain
principles which can promote a better milieu for a
patient to whom death is inescapble. Not only is a
better dying fostered, but the bereavement of survivors is apt to be shorter and less painful, while just
as sincere."

FOREMOST TO ME in the achievement of this
milieu is contacting a hospice organization.
Today, across the country are a growing number of
hospice programs. They range in scope from inpatient
facilities where people are admitted for care and treatment, to separate home-like units in hospitals, to hospice personnel working with patients within the regular
hospital structure. Here in Marin County, California,
we have services which provide care to patients who
have chosen to stay home. In Branford, the Connecticut
Hospice is building a prototype structure to augment
their current in-home services. Expected to be functional by 1980, the new facility is focus of attention by
hospice organizations world wide, eager to see what
fresh facets can be learned concerning care and treatment of terminal cancer patients.

Hospice, as a concept of humane treatment for the
dying, was re-established by Dr. Cicely Saunders with
the founding of St. Christopher's Hospice in London in
the late 1960's. Noted psychiatrist Elisabeth Kübler-
Ross carried the concept to the public through her
books, ON DEATH AND DYING; DEATH: THE FINAL

STAGES OF GROWTH, and the recently published, TO
LIVE UNTIL WE SAY GOODBYE.

Whether at home, in hospitals or convalescent facilities, hospice care involves a multi-disciplinary team addressing a full range of medical, psychological and social service needs of both patient and family during the illness, death and bereavement period. They aspire to lighten and deepen the end of life by reducing physical suffering and emotional anguish. Pain must be controlled. Only then can other needs and practical matters be handled.

"The hospice achievement is, in fact, a cause for general celebration," states Sandol Stoddard in her book, THE HOSPICE MOVEMENT: A BETTER WAY OF CARING FOR THE DYING. "It is one of the rare events of our time which is both fiscally creative and morally sound."

To me, being under hospice care meant becoming part of an expanded dedicated family. Most hospice organizations, certainly Hospice of Marin (HOM), deal not only with the patient but everyone involved. As mentioned, medical aspects do come first, working with and through the family physician. Next in importance, however, are feelings and attitudes of the entire family. It's in this open supportive available on-going dialogue that I found the greatest aid and comfort.

"They know what they're doing," writes James D. White, retired Associated Press correspondent and editor, whose wife, Jenifer, a HOM patient, died in October, 1977, "and do it in the belief that until prevention and/or cure for cancer becomes a reality, they have the nearest thing to an answer for the physical and mental agonies attending the disease. Employing expertise, the hospice staff minister to those suffering with a devotion and compassion which can scarcely be comprehended until it is experienced."

THERE ARE OTHER organizations offering services to improve the quality of life for the dying and their families. One such is Shanti, started by Charles Garfield, PhD, clinical research psychologist at University of California Medical Center Cancer Research Institute. With others who shared his concern, Dr. Garfield wanted an inexpensive, flexible way to deal with emotional needs of those facing life-threatening illness. Shanti-trained lay volunteers offering one-to-one counseling to patients is their answer. This free service to the San Francisco Bay Area community is available to a wide range of society; women frightened by the first lump discovered on a breast, those unable to resolve the pain of an old bereavement, husbands who can't deal with a spouse's life-shattering sickness. Shanti support is largely emotional, not encompassing the pain control and medical aspect basic to the hospice program. They do, however, help patients explore various avenues to alleviate suffering.

"Nothing Shanti does," says Katrin Achelis, one of the project's volunteer counselors speaking at a recent seminar, "wasn't in earlier times done for one another by members of a large extended family." Yet listening to clients, I sense that what Shanti provides is the big difference between facing the unknown alone or while supported by a caring, knowledgeable friend.

WHEREVER YOU LIVE, locate the resources in your community. Counterparts of the organizations I know here are developing across the country as established hospices and other groups offer training programs to healthcare professionals, clergy and the lay public. Services of such trained and concerned persons are becoming more and more available. It isn't necessary to deal with the demanding and frightening situation on your own. Seek and accept support.

From the moment the first HOM patient care coordinator came to interview my family, I never felt alone again. A trained person was always there, just a phone call away, to help with mother and perhaps more importantly in the long run, with the fears and inadequacies, sorrow and anger we were all experiencing. The HOM staff helped us face and accept the reality of death, to support and love mother while she prepared to die. And they formed, with us, in the richest, warmest sense, a team.

I DON'T WANT the children to remember me old and sick," said mother before HOM came on the scene. "I won't have them see me die. Put me someplace else before that happens."

In deference to her wishes, and because I couldn't face her dying myself at that point, I tried to protect the children, deprive them of experiencing what Dr. Kübler-Ross calls the necessary 'windstorms of life.' Luckily, HOM came to us and we faced this windstorm together. As it turned out, seeing her old and sick, having an active part in the reality of her death was the greatest gift she gave any of us.

Jim White says of his Jenifer, "It was happening, she couldn't prevent it yet she certainly could and did refuse to let it demoralize her. However, cancer is relentless. Courage alone is not enough. Hers was one of the most painful forms and not easily brought under control. But it was, and instead of dreading the agony of the next minute, hour, day or week, she was able to live to the fullest and most positive conclusion. Hospice made it possible for her courage to prevail. She remained entirely herself - her spirit, even her sense of humor, intact to the last moment of consciousness."

COST ALONE IS enough to make one choose
home-dying but that isn't the prime considera-
tion.   The horror of terminal illness has become [3]
not death itself but, according to Dr. Eric J. Cassell,
author of DEATH AND SOCIAL CHANGE, ". . . the
hospitalized dehumanized process of dying - alone,
away from family and friends - suffering, fearful, un-
certain, utterly dependent upon depersonalized technology, tied to tubes, tests, machines, unable to act
in one's own behalf. That's the nightmare; not simply
meeting death, but dying as an object, not a person."

The hospice concept doesn't condemn modern technology but works toward a renewal of values and attitudes often missing in this machine age by constantly
asking, "What is best for the patient?"

Special facilities and techniques are being developed
for care of the dying. Robert Kastenbaum,[4] superintendent of Cushing Hospital, Framingham, Massachusetts, and author of DEATH, SOCIETY AND HUMAN
EXPERIENCE, writes, "Administrators, attornies and
physicians - often cast as unfeeling villains in the dra-
ma of the deathbed scene - have been listening to what
nurses have to say and all have become more attentive
to what terminally ill and their families actually experience, expect and need. A new balance, a new inte-
gration is being developed."

All are working toward creation of a final environ-
ment in which those highest human qualities of patient, family and professional caregivers can be expressed. "We need to find ways," said Dr. Cassell,
"to put technology back in the service of patients, giving physicians definite choices for action, restoring
and fostering dignity and authenticity of people even in
the face of death."

3 , 4 - see page 62

Dr. Kübler-Ross states simply, "dying is only a nightmare if you make one of it. Total loving care is needed at the end of life just as it was in the beginning."

SUCH SENSITIVE care is available not exclusively at home. It can be found in those hospitals and nursing homes where the primary concern is what the patient needs and where family members are engaged in the care.

Family involvement is most important when a child is the hospitalized patient. Who can better bathe a child then the mother? Hold the child than the father? Siblings, too, can take part in the care. There is a natural danger ignoring - shutting out - your other children and putting all attention and energy on the dying child. It's almost impossible not to. Yet the other children have needs, fears, pain. When ignored, siblings not only develop problems, they become problems. Read the transformation of Jamie's brother when given responsibility for part of her care in TO LIVE UNTIL WE SAY GOODBYE. He changed from what Dr. Kübler-Ross termed "the worst brat, the most obnoxious child I've ever seen" into a proud concerned big brother.

"<u>Caring</u> care can be realized in a hospital and you, as the closest relative, can do a great deal to make it happen," advises my sister, Susan Shepard, rehabilitation nurse at a small hospital in Santa Rosa, California. "So if home-dying isn't possible or practical for any of a dozen reasons, don't feel guilty."

Jenifer White spent her final three months in the private room of a rest home. "With HOM's help,"writes Jim, "I was able to be with her night and day, around the clock, taking entire care of her needs. I felt after Jenifer died that no one anywhere could have done more. That's a good feeling, to know you've done your best."

FOR THE caregiver perhaps home-dying is most necessary if there is also a family to attend. Having everyone under one roof simplifies your role even in the complexity of final care. It's physically easier on you, emotionally, too, if you don't have to leave home - and its demands - to answer somewhere else, the additional needs of your dying intimate.

One problem in achieving home care arises when the patient is a parent firmly, often adamantly, entrenched in his or her own home. As this is not the home where you live, it creates a division of alliance. My mother had an apartment two miles away, a fine distance for privacy and independence during good health. In troubled times, it became a hardship all around. Many nights, in answer to a faint voice on the phone, I drove the short distance, hastily dressed, totally depressed. What would I find when I got there, how bad would it be? And I constantly worried that something so serious would happen that she'd be unable to reach the phone.

Eventually it became necessary to check on my way to school in the morning, shop for her (since the items were going to a different kitchen, it couldn't be part of my own shopping), stop again on my way home in the late afternoon, walk the dog, prepare dinner, ease her loneliness, get her ready for the night (much too early) and then go home and do many of the same things again for the rest of the family. Days were too long, nights too short. Many of the trips between the two homes I spent swearing, crying, praying. Looking back now, that was the hardest time.

WHAT WE DECIDED - demanded, actually - a month before we knew of the need for additional hospitalization which disclosed her terminal cancer,

was to bring mother - then 82 - home to live, antici-
pating years together. We closed her apartment and
divided her worldly goods except for special treasures
and dear necessities (her own bed and the Thaddeus
Welsh painting of Marin's tan hills at dusk!) kept to
furnish our big front bedroom. My husband Dick and I
moved down the driveway to take up residence in his
writing studio.

An outside door was installed in her room and wide
stairs built to accommodate her walker. Now she had
easy access to the garden and friends could visit without coming through the main house.

Unfortunately, not many sunny hours were spent in
the garden and not many friends had a chance to visit.
Mere weeks after the move she was in the hospital with
abdominal pains. An exploratory operation revealed
extensive cancer. Said the doctors, "There's nothing
we can do. It's just a matter of time - a short time."

At this point we made the decision to bring mother
home and keep her with us long as possible. Her room,
which she enjoyed so briefly, was ready. Dick installed
a doorbell on the wall by her bed. It chimed in the cottage. She called it her lifeline, summoning me at all
hours for reasons both trivial and serious. I came to
call it much worse!

That bell, however, gave her control and choice,
two extremely important faculties. According to Dr.
Weisman, "To ask for help in lessening pain is a good
way for patients to take charge of their own comfort
and clarity of mind, an option that is not insignificant
at a time when choices are few. Dying patients need to
feel a sense of management over at least part of their
plight. Otherwise, if control is gone, the disease takes
over completely."

AROUND THE clock care, when it reaches that point, is impossible to maintain on your own. We chose to have a licensed vocational nurse - a warm wonderful lady who became our friend - come in from 8 am to 4 pm each weekday. My daughter, then 20, was in charge from 4 to 6 pm and I took the nights. At times one son (17) gave the 10 pm medication, another son (15) gave the 6 am dosage, leaving me only the 2 am time. Usually I did all three plus in-between bell calls. Mother was not always cooperative with younger family members, to put it mildly. One of the ways she could still be "in charge" was to refuse to open her mouth for medication until she had quite a rhubarb going. She employed this power with a gleam in her eye!

Back then Dick was still working as a locomotive engineer running freight between Oakland and Roseville, California. He'd be gone for up to two days, then home for twelve hours, most of which he spent sleeping. His help, consequently, was more emotional support than physical aid with mother's care.

My sisters took turns coming 30 miles to share weekend duties, leaving me free to sleep through. What a blessing, uninterrupted sleep, reminiscent of the first night a new baby doesn't wake for a 2 am feeding.

Some sort of schedule must be developed to accommodate individual needs, to give structure, however flexible, to your nights and days. Time off, totally apart, is crucial to your well-being. To gain it, you need to ask for help, as I asked my children and sisters. This is not easy. I felt I 'should' be able to handle the situation by myself but quickly realized that mother's dying belonged to them, too.

Nancy Roach of Mill Valley, California, wrote THE LAST DAY OF APRIL, a "how we did it" story of the four and a half years her daughter Erin was dying of leukemia - from age $2\frac{1}{2}$ to 7. In this touching tribute to the bright spirit of a little girl, Nancy mentions the problem of seeking aid.

"My pride," she writes, "didn't allow me to ask for help when it seemed so obviously needed. I wanted the need to be seen. If I faced the same situation again, I would be open and ask for specific help. This would be a relief for those who wanted to support but didn't know how - and it would have diminished my own feelings of frustration."

MY CHILDREN WERE uneasy in the beginning if asked to stay alone with mother while I dashed out on a quick errand. They were afraid they'd do the wrong thing should an emergency arise in the ten minutes I was gone. This was one of the early fears discussed with the HOM team and their answers helped us all. There is very little you can do wrong, they assured us, when acting lovingly with a dying patient whose care has been established and pain control stabilized by professionals. Just being there, supportive and comforting, may be all that's needed - and that we are able to provide.

"But what if she dies?" asked my daughter Cathi. "I wouldn't know what to do." Again we talked to Hospice. Under these circumstances, death isn't likely to happen without gradual and increasingly plain signs. But if it does, it does. When Cathi realized she could neither cause nor prevent her grandmother's death, it was easier for her to be "on duty."

We moved our portable chemical potty from the camper to the bedside when trips down the hall to the bathroom were no longer feasible. Placed on cement blocks to make it bed height, the potty was convenient and inoffensively efficient.

My sons became adept at the strange ritual dance of

"stand, side-step, side-step, turn, sit," then the reverse back to bed. Remembering her help in toilet-training the little boys now grown to man-size, it was heart-tugging to see their strong arms around her fragile body, providing support on a three-step journey of utmost importance.

PEOPLE ARE ABLE to give if you're open and honest about your needs," wrote Stephanie Nowell whose husband Joe died in 1978. "I'm sure there are many people who didn't dream they could help anyone who was dying - and his family - as much as they were able to help us!"

Never underestimate the "bigness of little things." From friends, no gift is greater than showing they care. Ultimately, if they're able to understand how it is for you and can deliver the essense of that understanding with a caring act, even a small one, it makes a world of difference.

However, some people can't deal with dying. Perhaps their own unresolved fears get in the way. Whatever the reason, you'll find friends who aren't available. They won't telephone or write notes. They're busy denying the fact of death by shutting themselves off from your painful truth. Other friends will honestly say, "I can't, I simply can't." These may be willing to do special shopping or take the children on an outing, but they can't face you or the one who is dying. You don't have time or energy to dwell on this. Help will come from many sources, some unexpected; from neighbors, friends, supportive associates, strangers and family, far and near.

Accept this help and take precious time off. Freedom can be used in many healing ways, depending on your needs and resources. One friend took up jogging and ran until wonderfully tired. Another installed an exer-cycle and when the walls closed in rode uncounted miles. Several planned a weekly hour to kneel in church. Some prayed while weeding and watering the garden. There were those who meditated, did yoga or took exercise classes. Others hiked and found solace in the wonderful continuity of nature. I built a pond and waterfall in the lower garden, exhausting myself with huge rocks and cement, creating a structure of enduring beauty and satisfaction. Paint, write, sculpt, work with clay, find what you need.

Whatever you do during this mini-vacation, whether it's every day for a brief time or weekly, do it with your whole being. Come back refreshed, bringing strength and vitality with you.

This is an excellent time, also, to evaluate any strange new duties you'll have to assume when your partner dies. Marriage is - among other things - a system and when one spouse is no longer there, the system collapses. The effect of this collapse can be totally disruptive above and beyond the emotional turmoil caused by death of a beloved. Particularly true for long-married couples of generations when roles were clearly defined and the line between never crossed, the time to start preparing for this collapse is long before it happens.

Consider the husband who left alone can't open a can or boil water without burning it, to whom grocery shopping is worse than a trip to a strange planet, and who - with a degree in engineering - is mystified by the push-buttons on the washer and dryer. Or the wife who has never learned to drive, write a check or balance a bank book, who has never replaced a washer or driven a nail, who has not worked outside the home or earned money of her own. Part of a vanishing breed, they are totally complementary to each other, not really aware of the division of duties, and for decades have kept the

system beautifully functional. Now that comfortable
familiar structure is threatened with destruction by
the terminal illness of one spouse.

If you are in this position and in addition to impending loss and grief you'll need to assume duties foreign
to your current role, now is the time to start correct-
ive therapy. In areas where vast changes will be necessary, a little step taken now will prepare you for
that big jump later. Some of this you can map together
giving your intimate a sense of supporting you, playing
a continuing part in the system long as possible.

CONTINUITY IS an important element in a 'good
death.' Dr. Weisman said, "A dying person
resents being shut off from the daily flow of life.
Friends and family members who feel guilty about
being well, taking vacations, buying new clothes and
so on, are doing the patient a disservice when they
pretend they, too, have ceased living."
A recent magazine article[*] tells of Annie Kelley, who
is dying at home. She insists her four children go on
with their lives. "I don't want them to feel they have to
stay home every minute," she said. Annie remained
firmly planted in the middle of family life. She chose
to be downstairs where she wouldn't miss any of the
activity. "I don't want the children to tiptoe around
being quiet," she explained. "When they come home I
want them to yell, 'Hey, Mom,' and I want to be downstairs where I can hear them."
Let life continue to flow around the patient. Use the
living room, dining room, or as we did, a bedroom
with its own entrance for 'bedquarters.' We could have
locked and barred the front door during those weeks.
Everyone went in and out through 'Granny's room' saying hello and goodbye even when she no longer respond-
ed, touching her shoulder, her cheek, kissing her. We

* <u>Annie's Story</u>: Joan Libman, reprinted from March 13, 1979 issue
of Family Circle Magazine © 1979 THE FAMILY CIRCLE, INC.

took our meals on trays and sat near her, talking and laughing. Often she seemed to be ignoring us or unaware of our presence. Sometimes she'd suddenly smile and join the conversation. We kept her bedside radio going all the time, softly, audibly. Her little scruffy dog, Molly, spent hours on the bed where mother's hand could reach out and feel her. "Being home is wonderful," she often said. "I couldn't have my unsterile dog with me in a hospital." Again continuity; Molly had been her constant companion for years.

COMMUNICATION IS another of Dr. Weisman's elements of a 'good death.' "A dying person," he writes, "needs to talk about the individuality of impending death - what it's like, what is expected, what has been left undone."

You, too must talk, according to Elisabeth Kübler-Ross. "Tell everything you need to," she said, "especially the negative and unfinished things. Old resentments, get them out of the way on both sides. Then it's clear between you and saying, showing 'I love you' will be real, true."

Children, young children, when they are part of the patient's family, must be allowed - encouraged - to talk openly and honestly about feelings and permitted to express emotions relevant to death (or even those that seem to you irrelevant).

Shanti volunteers bring active listening to their clients as do hospice personnel. Nothing is more important, both to the patient and to you, the caregiver, than being able to communicate your feelings and thoughts.

"But how can I share my negative feelings with someone who is dying?" you ask. "How can I add that to other problems, real problems?" A hard question to answer: Maybe you can't. But if you stifle those

thoughts you soon become a walking emotional time-
bomb. Sharing with a Shanti counselor, or a hospice
person, can defuse the bomb and make it possible to
eventually share with your intimate those frightening
negative thoughts and feelings in a way that isn't
'dumping,' but rather a total honest communion.

Talking was one of the universal helps mentioned by
hospice survivors. Writes Stephanie Nowell, "I talked
about the problems. I needed to hear facts and bounce
feelings off others over and over until they became part
of my reality. I talked to Joe about his feelings and expressed mine. Sometimes I was very angry with Joe
and confronted him with my anger."

"We were able," says Ruth Goodyear about her husband Lowell's dying, "to discuss everything and anything and were closer to each other than ever. We
laughed and joked and cried."

BUT WHAT IF you're dealing with a person who
refuses to accept dying or to mention death? In
the face of overwhelming medical evidence, the patient's faith in 'beating this thing' precludes any discussion. How can you know where belief stops and
bravado begins? Or what panic lies under that desper-
ately confident surface? How much of this denial is a
necessary coping mechanism? We all deny segments
of our reality at times. It's a normal function, a defense used while mustering forces to face a situation.
Where is the line, and what can you do?

Any terminal patient has undoubtedly lived with the
knowledge of death day and night for longer than you
think, for longer in all probability than either you or
the doctor. Whether it can be expressed or not is another thing.

Recently I was one of the speakers at a Hospice
Training Seminar after dinner meeting. Two of the

other speakers were father and son whose wife/mother had died a scant three months before. Obviously a close and articulate family, they had nonetheless not talked together about her impending death. Yet the feeling was there, as they expressed it to us that evening; on one level she knew they knew she knew so there was no reason for explicit words. All the understanding and support was implicit in their total relationship.

But, I continued asking myself even as they were answering the question, why, if they were that comfortable and that close, didn't they go one step farther and check it out? Might it not have been better if they had been explicit? Who knows?

TO ME IT is somewhat comparable to staying with a traveler aboard ship until the "All ashore" sounds, then watching the vessel depart without ever mentioning the journey, the destination, or saying, "Bon voyage." And another part of me says, "But to be there, to stand by, doesn't that show you know he's departing? Isn't that a form of goodbye?"

One striking feature of both Hospice and Shanti is that neither imposes "shoulds" on anyone. They allow space for individual needs, beliefs and responses. This is an attribute I need to cultivate!

Discussing death, even - or especially - when you know you are dying isn't something everyone is able to do. "You can open walnuts," stated Charlie Garfield at the Shanti seminar I attended, "but you can't open up people. They, dying or not, will be consistent with who and what they are. Communication can't be forced. If you try, you're likely to close it off."

You can hope with them that, yes, they just may "lick it," they may be able to take that trip in the spring. But you need to still honor your own knowledge and understanding of the situation. Keep the conversation open-ended. Ask, "What if. . . ?" Watch for non-verbal clues that might give you an opening. Dr. Kübler-Ross has patients, particularly children, draw quick spontaneous pictures, then talks with them about what each picture says.

I RECENTLY VISITED a widow whose husband died of cancer after six months of downhill fighting. He maintained until the end that he was getting better. His defenses made him unapproachable. Nor was she willing to accept his dying so she too was silent. (If we don't mention or acknowledge death, maybe it'll go away!) She said to me during our visit, "Now I'm sorry. I wish I'd talked to Charles about his dying." It's a special sorrow to her that she didn't. There are so many things she wishes they had shared while there was time!

If you can reach an organization such as Shanti or if you are involved with a hospice group, their expertise in active listening, their knowledge, will be a help, a support to you as mentioned. Perhaps this will make it possible to communicate with your dying intimate before time runs out and you find yourself, like my friend, with regrets for things left unsaid, now lost forever.

It's unnecessary to talk constantly about death, but meeting it honestly is important. "The more I brought my thoughts and feelings to the conscious level," said Nancy Roach, "the easier the subject of death was to think and talk about. It was like flexing an unused muscle. As time went on our conversations became more advanced."

Until this experience with my mother, I wasn't able to talk comfortably about death. Something in our culture and my upbringing made the subject, if not totally

taboo, at least somewhat improper. Embarrassing to
mention, uncomfortable to think about, death was a
fact to be skirted, ignored, especially when with someone who was dying. Yet there it lurked, dark and
frightening in the corners of our minds.

TEN YEARS AGO my brother Bill died of cancer.
He was 45 years old, had spent six months in
chemotherapy, and was hospitalized in early December.
Both mother and I visited him daily, watched him
struggle with pain that had to be borne until time for
the next knock-out medication. I remember looking at
his sweating face and checking my watch. "Only 30
more minutes. Hang on."
     We knew he was dying. He, I presume, knew he
was dying. Yet we still played out the farce of, "When
I get out of here. . ." "In the spring when you're
stronger. . ." Never once did we say what we were
feeling or give him an opening to say what he felt!
     We had to leave when visiting hours were over on
the afternoon of a gray wet Christmas Eve. "See you
soon," we said. He died alone before his next medication. Even now it hurts that I didn't say goodbye, didn't
talk about his feelings, didn't say, "I love you. I'll
miss you."
     It was even harder on mother. She was filled with
'if only's' for the rest of her life. Perhaps that's one
reason her own death eight years later was so different.

DYING IS BY its very nature self-centered. The
world folds in, smaller and smaller, as a person makes ready to die. It becomes nearly impossible
for you, the caregiver, to function on a standard time-
table. This was hard for me to understand or accept.
Medication to prevent pain went on around the clock,
every four hours; that was a constant. But to mother,

slowly separating from our reality, time had an entirely different aspect, a strange warp.

At first, in the interest of efficiency and convention, I tried to 'straighten her out.' This was frustrating for both.

"No, Mother," I would say patiently (or impatiently depending on the time of day and my energy level), "you've only been asleep a few minutes. It's still evening, not morning. You need dinner, not breakfast." Or, "Who ever heard of <u>lunch</u> at 3 am?"

How futile! How foolish! Dr. William M. Lamers, Jr., medical director of HOM, a tender bear of a man with a deep vibrant voice, talked to me about what I was building into a problem.

"Go with her," he said gently. "Accept her inner signals. She doesn't need your clock." So borrowing his acceptance and compassion, I allowed her the special reality of a diminished world.

I ALSO LEARNED the strange art of Liliputian cooking. What she wanted, she wanted RIGHT NOW. Some dishes could be prepared in advance and doled out by scant spoonfuls on demand. Jello and custard served well here. But what of a sudden desire for potato soup, oatmeal mush, or pea soup and mashed potatoes with gravy? A teaspoon of 'instant' whatever (and almost everything comes in instant form these days), mixed with hot water, a dab of butter, a dollop of cream and a smidge of salt or sugar did the trick. She enjoyed the two or three tiny bites she was able to down. But only if the meal appeared within minutes! Otherwise, the desire was gone, the want forgotten. I really hustled and took creative joy in concocting minuscule portions of whatever she demanded and getting it to her before she switched desires.

For her constant thirst, tiny ice cubes were easier

to handle than a glass of water. A spoonful of ice
cream or sherbet was sometimes welcome but her
sense of taste had deteriorated to the point she could
hardly tell 'goodies' from plain ice so we didn't usually
bother. Actually, drinks were harder than food to prepare without waste. I'd always announce, "I'm going to
make Granny a milk shake. Come and drink it!" Then
I could pour her two sips into a tiny glass and hand the
rest to a hollow-legged growing boy.

Her wants were simple. But they were constant!

LOOKING BACK now on those final weeks of mother's long life, I, too, wonder how we made it.
Other survivors share this amazement at the stretching
of limits to meet needs and demands. Broken sleep,
long hours, emotional tension, the immediacy of the
moment! It's not easy. But it isn't all hard, either.
There come, I remember, flashes of such beauty and
sharing, such spirituality, such joy, that approaching
death loses its terror and your imminent loss becomes
shadowy.

Mother was a totally different person during her
last weeks than anyone I'd ever known. Of course
physically she was changed. From a commanding
regal person with a positive manner - efficient, organ-
ized, in control - she had dwindled to a tiny waif with
a husky whisper and a smile of incredible sweetness.
But the change was more than physical. I've heard
other survivors say of their intimate, "He was himself
right to the last moment." Mother wasn't. Or she was
a self we'd never been privileged to know. Before, it
was difficult for her to verbally express love, to be
soft and tender. Now, she opened her arms wide to us
and said, "I love you." Strange, wonderful words from
a woman who couldn't say them most of her life.

"Love," she whispered now, "is the answer, the

only important thing. It's all that matters." Not money, not health, not even life; just love.

Heartbreaking though it may be, in a way it's easier to care for someone who doesn't remind you of the person they were. I knew this was my mother. I could tell for sure when I looked deep in her eyes where the strength still shone. But most of the time she was a dear stranger for whom I had great tenderness and deep responsibility. Mother, the grand demanding lady who had been around (and bossed me around!) all my life, was already gone. This, I saw, was a first step in the impending total separation, a preparation for what was coming. But our precious truthful moments, speaking of love, of answers to the eternal riddle of life, hearing her hoarsely whisper these words, brought us closer than we ever before allowed ourselves to be.

SEPARATION, loss and grief are all intrinsic in the dying of a loved one. How you express these emotions to each other is important. Dr. Weisman mentions composure as one of the essentials to a 'good death.' Not a stiff-upper-lip denial of reality but what the dictionary defines as "self-possession, calmness." So along with honest communication of feelings and thoughts between you and the person dying, both need to maintain a self-possessed calm, not giving in to excessive emotions or burdening the other with histronics.

One friend, at times when his composure was about to slip, took a shower and cried - shouted - under the private screen of water. He was extremely clean during those final weeks of his wife's too short life!

YOU NEED NOT suppress feelings. It's the difference between saying, even with a catch in your

voice and tears in your eyes. "I feel awful! I don't
know what I'll do without you. " Or flinging yourself on
the bed and sobbing, "Why, why, why? I can't stand
it! I can't bear it! What'll become of me without
you? I'll die too! I will, I will!"

The first allows the patient to reply, "I know. Leaving you alone is my worst worry too, " followed by a
discussion, however tearful but still composed, of ways
you can cope alone, of what your resources are, emotional and financial, of what changes you can start initi-
ating now. This facing reality can make you both feel
better. Perhaps here you could together make one specific plan, something special you're going to do after
the death. My sister and I arranged a weekend of inten-
sive massage at Esalen Institute in Big Sur, California.
We sent our reservations a month in advance for a date
which turned out to be two weeks after mother's death.
She even paid the fee, one of her final gifts.

The latter outburst - and there are times, many
times, when you'll feel this way - is best saved for the
sheltering walls of the shower! I found driving the car
was excellent for expressing uncontrolled emotions.
It's a relief to scream, shout obsenities, swear, sob
and finally run out of steam, all without assaulting another ear or burdening another soul. I've been asked if
this is compatible with safe driving. Probably not; I
usually pulled off the road at the height of the storm.
But you can physically concentrate on driving while
emotionally letting go, particularly late at night on
straight and quiet roads.

ONE PROBLEM I brought with me to the situation.
Unlike my husband, who can be asleep in 18 sec-
onds, I have a hard time letting go of consciousness,
turning off the movie screen of my mind. The more
that's going on in life, the more I need sleep, the hard-

er it is for me to give in. Yet when the alarm is going to ring again in a few hours for the next medication, it's urgent to go instantly to sleep.

Dr. Lamers advised self-hypnosis which eventually might have worked but didn't in the time I had. However, my sister Susan, half-jokingly, gave me a temporary and simple solution when I phoned her in desperation.

"Get the mixings for brandy alexanders," she suggested. "Make a batch and put it in the refrigerator with a glass. Every time the bell rings, pour one. Drink half. Go take care of Mom. Come back and drink the other half. Get in bed and sleep."

It worked! And mother didn't live long enough for me to become a lush.

CLOSURE IS THE last essential element in the 'good death' mentioned by Dr. Weisman. It's been happening in bits and pieces since that long ago acceptance of the fact of dying. Even before that, in such acts as making a will, providing life insurance, discussing plans and desires with family and close friends, final closure was being facilitated.

In Jenifer White's last month at home she went through the whole house, with Jim pushing the wheelchair, deciding all the things that had to be decided after 44 years together.

"This," wrote Jim, "made it possible for an innately tidy person to feel that her affairs were in some sort of order. It made it possible for me to know her wishes and carry them out later without having to guess about them."

Mother had done the same thing with her possessions when we moved her home to live with us. And over the years she'd made specific arrangements for her death to save us from facing decisions on such problems in a

time of stress. She had even prepaid everything possible!

Always mother had said, "No funeral. Not even a
memorial service. Just cremation, quick and clean."
But as death drew near, she understood our need for
closure, too, and admitted a memorial service would
be all right with her. In fact, she got behind planning
it with a flash of her old organizational ability!

DURING THE NEXT to last week, she greeted me
each morning with the name of someone she
wanted to see once more in order to say goodbye. I'd
phone and explain the invitation. Difficult as it was,
most of them came. A heroic amount of composure
was displayed in that sunny room. It was harder on the
visitor than us. We'd been living with and talking about
mother's approaching death for weeks. Such honesty
was overwhelming to suddenly confront in a brief almost casual visit. Mother was very clear in what she
wanted to say. It was, "I love you. Goodbye." She also
wanted to reminisce. A little "Remember when . . ,"
usually something funny. With my ex-husband, father of
my five children, she wanted to forgive him for what
she imagined he'd done decades before and to tell him
everything had turned out all right - he, the children,
me, life - and, yes, to say, "I love you."

IN THE FINAL week mother was more 'there' than
here, touching a reality that wasn't ours. She sat
propped up by pillows looking into a space we couldn't
see. Often during these days she included us in three-
way conversations with others, or reported what she
was seeing. Once it was her deceased sister, a commanding dowager who during her life always wore black
and white, pearls, veiled hats, gloves.

"Look at Rill," chortled mother, "in a bright red

dress!" She was really amused at this unexpected flamboyance, and irritated with me for not seeing her, too. Other long-gone people were also there. "Can't you see them?" she asked.

At a recent seminar when I was sharing this story someone said, "Do you think she was hallucinating?" "No," I answered, "I think they were all there at the foot of her bed. I just couldn't see them." I felt their presence through mother's obvious participation in a reality beyond our realm.

One day when she brought her attention back to Susan and me she said with total wonderment, "Dying is the experience of a lifetime." When we asked for details (In what way? How come? What do you mean?), she smiled like a child hugging a secret and whispered, "You'll see."

Another time quite crossly she demanded, "How long do I have to wait? Let me go!"

"We're not holding you," Sue replied softly. "You can die whenever you're ready."

Our goodbyes said, we actually gave her permission to go, feeling this was an important act. Sometimes, through desperate love, one holds to a dying intimate with strong invisible bonds. Susan, in her hospital work, often asks family members, "Have you said goodbye? Have you told her it's okay to die?" Usually they reply, shocked, "Oh, I can't!" but later are able to do just that to set their intimate free. A peaceful death, in many instances, happens soon after as though that permission was a missing key.

SO IT WAS with mother. One by one she tied the loose ends. One by one she cut the bonds. Then she quietly waited.

Nancy Roach told of the last days of Erin's short life, so exactly like the last days of mother's long life.

Erin wanted her parents nearby but no longer wished to
be talked to, would brush away a touching hand. When
the separation was complete, Erin gently died.
   As did my mother.
   As did the intimates of my hospice friends.
   As will your beloved patient.

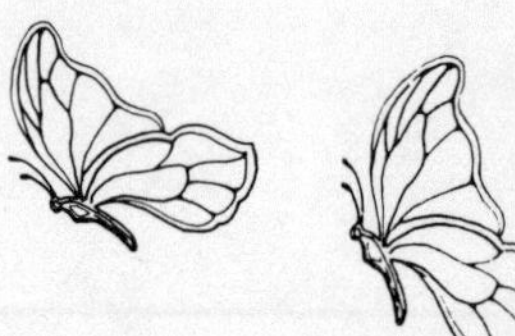

D EATH IS the final moment
of this existence for
the dying. For you, the
living, it is also
a new beginning. . .

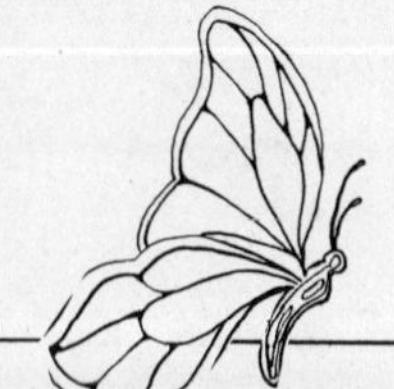

... and After

THERE ARE over ten million widows and nearly two million widowers in the United States today. Last year 390,000 Americans died of cancer, about one tenth of them children. Another 37,000 people were killed in automobile accidents.

Unique as your grief is, you can see you are not alone. If you played an involved part in the dying of your intimate, you are one of the more fortunate. Everything you did during that difficult time is making this moment easier to bear. Nothing anyone says can remove your loss or alleviate your pain any more than words, however wise and comforting, changed the fact of death. But knowledge can help you face what you're experiencing with understanding and perspective.

What each person brings to grief is, as with everything else, the sum total of past experience. You deal with current loss based on your whole body of accumulated knowledge. If, as a child, you were allowed to feel Elisabeth Kübler-Ross's 'windstorms of life' under the sheltering tutelage of a loving adult, if - all along the way - you've faced, dealt with and accepted the vicissitudes of relationships, you have a background to deal with your new loss. Not that this makes it any easier; it just means you have tools as part of your make-up and are not totally defenseless.

GRIEF IS THE reaction to loss of a person or thing to which we have become attached," writes psychiatrist Colin Murray Parkes,[5] author of BE-REAVEMENT: STUDIES OF GRIEF IN ADULT LIFE. "It is a natural and normal reaction with a natural form and sequence.

"Grieving," he continues, "is a way of relearning the world. It takes time. And because no two relation-ships are alike and no two worlds the same, each per-son goes through it in his or her own way."

Psychiatric research indicates that attempts to deny or avoid grief are potentially harmful. It's important for people who suffer loss to accept the need to grieve and for those in a helping position to encourage the be-reaved to express these feelings. When delayed grief begins to emerge, and it always does in one form or another, it will be more painful and disruptive than if it had been fully expressed at the time of loss.

When death comes to your intimate at home, there are numerous details to take care of immediately, mun-dane routine matters, different than in a hospital where others assume command. If you did your 'homework' well, these will be almost automatic. I remember ask-ing the hospice coordinator far in advance, "What do I do when mother dies?" She outlined if for me —one, two, three. . . - so I knew the exact procedure for our case; who to phone first, what to do.

Whoever has been your contact, counselor, confi-dante will come to the house immediately when notified. That person will call the attending physician and funeral director should you want, and wait with you until the body has been removed. (What a large emptiness that leaves!) Those who are gathering around will - as they have so many times before - encourage you and family

5 - see page 62

members to express what you are feeling, helping you get in touch with what's happening, reaffirming with all of you the worth of your contribution in caring for your beloved patient.

A 'GOOD death,' according to Dr. Weisman, always seems to happen at the right time. Susan and I were both with mother at three o'clock on a warm Sunday afternoon when she peacefully died. Chiming of seminary bells on a nearby hill made it seem exquisitely 'right.' Susan, a nurse, knew the physical things to do and efficiently did them; shutting mother's eyes, laying her down, closing her mouth, arranging her arms. Mother looked as if quietly sleeping, yet the stillness was so profound there was a strange difference. She was gone.

Moments later, we phoned her regular non-hospice doctor as prearranged. He, of course, was not on duty as it was Sunday. The doctor who appeared at the house a short time later was a stranger to us. He referred to mother, whose name was Marian Rattray, as "Mrs. Crabtree." This, coupled with the sudden almost giddy realization that the long struggle was over, made us both giggle hysterically. There's a rush of relief when a long-anticipated death occurs, a thankful release that in our case was almost intoxicating.

The doctor, whose name I promptly forgot in retaliation for his gaucherie, called the funeral home where mother had already made arrangements. The undertaker, slightly confused as to identity of deceased (he had no record of 'Crabtree' and hadn't understood our off-stage correction during the phone conversation) arrived in due time with his helper and a long black car. Maybe he wasn't typical but his manner made me wonder if the unctiousness of people in his profession is an inborn trait or something they're encouraged to learn.

Having spent a month honestly facing death and talking about it on many levels with everyone involved, it was difficult to relate to this stranger's oblique, veiled questions, his euphemistic phrases.

Susan and I felt useless and unnecessary while they silently did what had to be done to mother in the room where we'd spent so many busy hours. We hovered just out of sight until he coughed gently to attract our attention.

"She's ready. Do you want to say anything?"

"Thank you, no," answered Sue, appropriately prim and subdued. "We've already said it all."

I DIDN'T WATCH as they took her down the steps built for her use just three months before. I looked briefly, then turned away as they slid the stretcher into the back of the hearse. The door swung quietly shut. A very final act, it made me feel cut-off, bereft.

Susan asked to be alone to strip the bed and room of all the accouterments of dying; to dust, spray, polish and vacuum. I picked and arranged fresh flowers for the cleaned room, then made phone calls to key relatives who would spread the word. We firmed the date for the memorial service at the church so such information could be imparted with the same phone call. We talked to HOM to bring them up to date and to say that, so far, we were coping well and didn't need help.

I added final statistics to the newspaper notices I'd already written, clipped them to glossy prints we had chosen to have made (who is this smiling lady with the coronet braid and strong face?), and slipped them into addressed envelopes for delivery to papers the next day.

Suddenly mother had been dead two hours. For the first time in months we had nothing, absolutely nothing

to do. What we did next was appropriate for us. My
sons were away, husband Dick was working on the
railroad, daughter Cathi involved in a previous engagement. Susan and I dressed up, took the last of mother's ready cash, and went out to a special dinner in her
honor.

WE HELD A memorial service the following Sat-
urday afternoon, gathering after the church
ceremony with relatives and friends in the lower garden by the new pond and waterfall. Here we talked
with one another, spontaneously bringing from our
store of memories facets of mother's long active life.
She was more 'real' that day in our words and laughter
then she'd been for a long time. It was a poignant celebration of a special passage.

How you commemorate the death of your intimate
is, hopefully, something you discussed together in de-
tail long before the fact so that decisions were made
and plans laid. Then, as with us, you'll be able to put
things into motion with minimal effort. What you do
depends on personal choice, family tradition, religious
customs and sociological pressure. But most of all, it
must serve your needs.

Vanderlyn R. Pine,[6] associate professor of sociology at State University in New York, wrote in his book,
CARETAKER FOR THE DEAD, "The funeral reinforces the bereaved person's role in society while af-
firming the social order itself. It also affirms family
cohesiveness with the extended family, conveying a
sense of being part of a larger whole. In this way, a
funeral demonstrates the 'roots' of the individual, the
family and society."

THERE HAS BEEN much said against funeral
practices in the years since Jessica Mitford's

1963 best seller, THE AMERICAN WAY OF DEATH, in
which she castigated funeral directors for their meth-
ods and faulted them for their extravagances. However,
a funeral or memorial ceremony serves a three-fold
function. It is, simultaneously, a rite of separation, a
rite of transition and a rite of incorporation. First,
the service separates the living from the dead and provides for disposal and commitment of the body. Second,
it allows public acknowledgement of your new role,
changing caregiver to bereaved - wife to widow, husband to widower, child to orphan. Here, also, the offering of condolences reinforces the reality of death.
And finally, it symbolically - in any religious ceremony - incorporates the dead into the 'other world.'

All this is more important than it may seem to you
now. I know from sad experience, or lack of it, at the
time my brother died. Perhaps because it was Christmas, perhaps because his widow - unable to face him
during those final days - had flown north to be with her
family for the holidays and to grieve in private, whatever the reason, we had no services to mark his death.
Nothing to allow friends and relatives to gather, to say,
"He lived, he died. We remember and honor that memory. We're saddened he's no longer with us." Because
that didn't happen, I still cry at unexpected moments.
There was no closure, no completion. We missed a
second chance to say goodbye.

So such services are important. They mark a dis-
tinct ending, a period. After that, no matter how deep
your sorrow, how fresh your grief, you face a new beginning. And you go on - step by step, day by day.

IT IS POSSIBLE to make your own goodbyes, however, if circumstances prevent participation in
conventional ceremonies or if you were apart at the
time of death and are experiencing a sense of incom-

pleteness.

Dr. Lamers tells of a family whose husband/father was killed in an accident far from home. No service was held and as time went on, the need for closure became apparent, especially with the children.

As a family, they planned a simple private goodbye. Each person, even the youngest child, brought two things for the missing father, lost husband; a note (the littlest drew a picture) and an item, chosen with care. Gathering together in the backyard of the family home, they silently placed letters and treasures in a special box which was then buried under a big shade tree. They cried a little, hugged each other, remembering the man they were honoring, and felt a gentle completion.

My friend Joyce Pederson and her daughter were hiking in the High Sierras shortly after the death of Joyce's father. Axel had been a rugged outdoorsman and had, years before, taught Joyce to ski close to where they now walked this hot summer day. Suddenly Joyce realized it was the time and place to say goodbye to Axel. "I just <u>knew</u>," she told me later. "We hadn't planned it but everything felt right."

As they climbed to the peak of the wind-swept mountain, both Lyn and Joyce began to collect items along the way; a slalom pole, the base of a ski pole, momentos of winters past and a sport Axel loved. When they reached the peak, where rugged stunted trees gave witness to the constant wind, Joyce moved granite rocks to form a small cairn. To this they added the poles and other broken items. Lyn took the scarf from around her neck and tied it to the slalom stick. "Looking out over that measureless distance I felt close to Axel," reported Joyce. "It was easy to say goodbye."

Not so for my sister, Marianne Shepard. A lady of action rather than words, she wasn't comfortable talking to mother as Susan and I were, nor could she ex-

press love as easily. Yet she did something for mother
the rest of the family couldn't do. Her declaration of
caring, her special goodbye, was to promise a home
for Molly, the untidy little dog Sue and I viewed with
distaste. In saying to mother, "I'll take Molly,"
Marianne said everything: 'I know you're dying. This
is goodbye. I'm doing what I can to show I care.'

Mother was able to relax with a real worry checked
off her list. Marianne's goodbye was a reassuring act
at a time when words, for her, were meaningless.

PATIENTS WHO die a 'good death'," wrote Dr.
Weisman, "leave a legacy for survivors in that
mourning is shorter, less painful, with fewer recrim-
inations and much relief. Remembrance is then a tribute, not an emotional burden." Certainly if you aided
in the achievement of this 'good death,' you're steps
ahead of those who suffer the shock of sudden unexpected bereavement.

"We realized," said Nancy Roach, "that hard as it
would be to lose Erin someday, it would be easier
knowing we'd done all we could. Sometimes we over-
acted by wanting to give her the world and all its treasures. Then we realized that to a child the 'world' is
the security of a loving family."

I don't equate the grief of losing and elderly ready-
to-die parent with that of losing a vital partner who a
short time before seemed healthy. The shattering im-
pact of that I can only imagine. And I can't stretch my
imagination to encompass the loss of a child. Such pain
is beyond my ken, like standing on the edge of a preci-
pice in total darkness. But I do know the weeks of
preparation (which for some stretches into months and
even years), of doing everything we possibly could for
mother, of saying goodbye, left us the sense of personal victory and accomplishment. Our sorrow wasn't

tainted with remorse for words unsaid, guilt for acts
undone. Regret is powerful and dehabilitating, as is
guilt. Involvement in the process of your intimate's
dying alleviates the burden of such negative feelings.

REACTION TO LOSS by death usually follows a
predictable pattern," wrote Dr. Parkes, "in the
course of which the bereaved make real inside themselves a situation that is already an established reality
outside."

This pattern (see diagram) happens in whole or part
again and again, triggered by holidays, birthdays, an-
niversaries. In looking at the cycle, keep in mind that
it is merely a diagram and not a road map or prototype
of the 'right' way. There is no one perfect pattern of
grief. In fact, 'normal' encompasses the entire gamut
and, like the stages of dying made famous by Dr. Kübler-Ross, is a graphic representation of thousands of
statistics depicting diversity of response. But people
are not statistics. No one will experience all these
reactions nor will these feelings happen in a neat pre-
scribed sequence.

I heard Dr. Kübler-Ross at a recent lecture rue the
day she delineated those stages of dying. She feels they
get misinterpreted and misused.

"A nurse," she said, "glances into a room, sees the
the patient is obviously mad. 'Good!' she thinks, 'coming right along.' She writes on the record, 'Patient
reached angry stage at 3 pm' and lets it go at that. The
patient, truly angry, is furious because the food is rot-
ten or because his bed needs changing and nobody's
paying attention, not - at this moment - because he's
dying!

"Don't use labels as a crutch," she cautioned.
"Check everything out."

The same applies to the following diagram:

CYCLE OF GRIEF

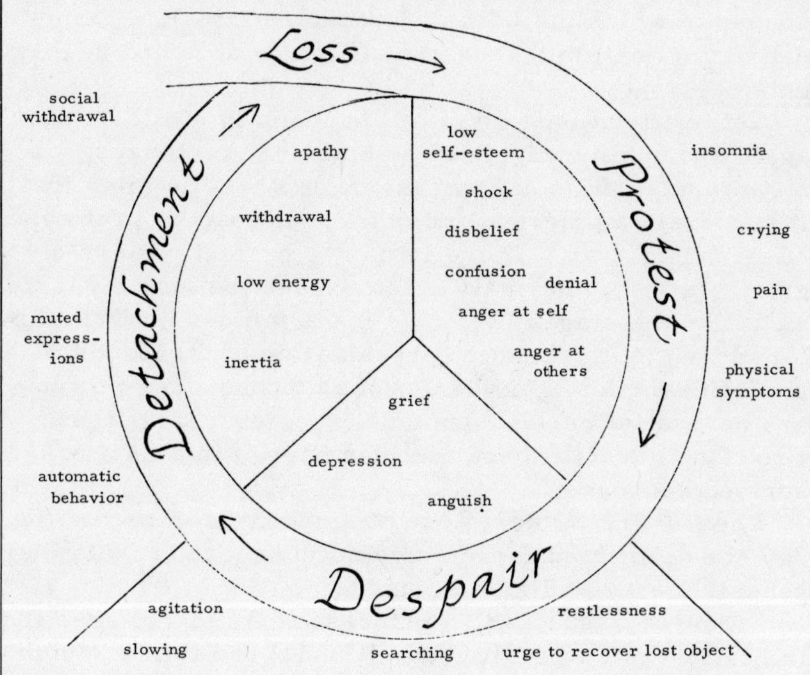

- William Lamers, Jr., MD

IN TALKING OF the grief process at a HOM bereavement lecture, Wendy Foster, a marriage family child counselor (MFCC) says, "Loss is a wound. It needs air to heal. If covered up, it festers." While you can avoid the cycle, shut off or skip parts of it, there is no escape in the process of grieving. "It's wiser," she adds, "to let it happen. Go with the feelings." Then hour by hour, day by day, imperceptibly there will come a lessening of intensity.

Wendy also points out that among the 'normal' feelings experienced by bereaved are frightening thoughts of suicide ("There's nothing left to live for. I might as well be dead!"), anger ("How could you die and leave me like this? How could God - if there is one - do this to me?"), guilt ("It was my fault. I should have done better."), relief (both anger and relief are likely to trigger more guilt; "I shouldn't feel this way. I'm bad.") and the universal phenomenon of visions.

Dr. Parkes reports, "At times bereaved people will experience a strong sense of presence of the deceased. Sights and sounds may be misinterpreted as indicating a return and vivid dreams occurring in a half-waking state may be recalled as apparitions."

THIRTY-SEVEN YEARS ago, in the first May of American involvement in World War II, my young fighter pilot fiance was killed. In spite of the almost universal premonition of receiving such word from the War Department, I was totally unprepared for the telegram. (Not Russell, not us!) Dealing with this type of death is complicated by its lack of closure. One can delude oneself for a long time that the news is false, the facts wrong, that it didn't really happen! Such a death, too, is completely removed from daily life. It was only the nebulous future and shining dreams that were destroyed with him.

But as I slowly came to believe those stark words,
". . . killed in a plane crash on the 25th of May. . ,"
two episodes happened that are as clear today as they
were then although other events of that long ago time
have blurred into a shadowy conglomerate.

The first incident took place while driving with a
friend who had taken me to a movie. Suddenly I was a-
ware of the individual unique hair tonic and after shave
lotion mixture that was unmistakably Russell's. I was
sure he was present in the car! It was strangely reassuring, making him seem more truly dead, and at
the same time, not entirely lost.

The second experience happened, as Dr. Parkes
suggested such events do, in a half-sleeping state. I
awoke and knew the weight and warmth of Russell's
hand over my heart. I raised my hand, placed it on the
spot and felt, not my own flesh, but a density of space,
hand-shaped, that I couldn't penetrate.

Two small happenings but in my confused and resist-
ant state of mind they offered proof of the death I was
denying, plus, in a strange mystical way, a measure of
comfort. My 'misinterpreted presence of the deceased'
in both cases, helped me acknowledge the reality of a
death that happened half a world away and accept it.

WITH PASSAGE OF time, such 'sensings' disap-
pear, intensity and frequency of grief pangs di-
minish. The bereaved weaves back and forth, from
protest through despair to detachment, through healing
and finally out on the other side with a recommitment
to life and a return to normalcy.

"How long?" you may ask. "How long does it take?"

A recent telephone conversation with a dear friend
turned, as it always does, to memories of her busband,
Haskell Weaver, who died eight years ago. "Never a
day," she said, "never an hour goes by I don't miss

him. It's still so hard!"

Leah is, outwardly, 'recommitted to life and return to normalcy' in that she's a functioning individual, working, making decisions. Her married son and delightful daughter-in-law live nearby. They just made her a first-time grandmother. That helps. But being unable to share the wonder of a new generation with the baby's grandfather leaves, as do so many things, an aching hole. And 'normalcy' to her will never be a half-empty house, an unshared bed or life's absurdities unmarked by a well-remembered laugh.

DICK'S BROTHER, Steve Murdock, noted political writer, died in October 1977, three weeks after my mother, ending a year of critical ill health from cirrhosis of the liver. His widow, Evelyn recently wrote, "We are all different and must each find our way through death, sorrow, grief. I, for instance, could sleep in the same bed in which Steve died. I could remain in the same house. Others can't.

"I know it's important to accept death," she continued, "before you can begin to live a new life. Changing those things that make it seem the person is only away and coming home soon is important. But it is also important not to make any big changes. You can't run from the reality of that death. Stay and work it through. Wait until you know who you are and where you want your life to go."

Long ago, in the middle of my third pregnancy - the one that produced our only daughter - I was trying to decide what to do with the messy muddle life had become: File for divorce or try again with an angry, estranged husband? Move or stay put? Farm out the children and get a job or stay home and go on welfare? On and on, around and around! These alternatives I poured out, more than slightly hysterical, to my wonderful understanding doctor during a monthly checkup.

He, a big craggy Texan, looked down at me and drawled, "Honey, no pregnant lady should ever try to make big decisions." Then he smiled and patted me gently. "Just keep your mind a swingin' door," he said. I've hugged that phrase, a talisman, to my heart a hundred times. In any stressful situation it is calming as oil on water. Try it. You can't be frantic when your mind's a swingin' door.

GRIEF AND MOURNING," writes George E. Williams, associate professor of psychiatry at University of Minnesota, "particularly in the depression stage, are frequently accompanied by pains in the chest or throughout the entire body. One of the most common symptoms is throat pain, which can be a defense against talking about feelings and is usually related to an inability to share with and feel comforted by supportive people."

Those who have been involved in the long dying of an intimate often fail to realize the toll taken on their bodies. It's easy to expect too much of yourself in the days, weeks and months after the death. Like getting back strength following an operation or serious illness, it is a slow gradual process.

Although you may appear to have accepted death intellectually, both psychologically and physiologically these painful feelings may continue. Resolution often takes considerable time, but the beginning of this phase, according to Dr. Williams, is apparent when the bereaved begins to recall and talk about pleasant and happy memories of the loved one who died.

Evelyn Murdock wrote about remembering. "Another thing that helped," she said, "were memories I had of our life together. Not memories to dwell on but to be thought of with happiness. It isn't necessary to forget.

It is necessary to put memories into perspective. I can now see a beautiful sunset with more joy because of Steve and that's a memory I cherish."

Whenever we visit Evelyn much of our time is spent reliving earlier days when the four of us were together, or sharing separate memories from our individual reservoirs. Once again, talking is excellent therapy.

Evelyn is a realist, a strong capable lady. She's also fortunate, like my friend Leah, in having children and grandchildren nearby plus the demands of an interesting job. It's been nearly three years now since Steve's death. She still has moments when some reminder triggers pangs of grief or an episode of sadness. She probably always will. But Evelyn Murdock has made a full circle and is, she feels, 'through it.'

KATHRYN Morgan Ryan, widow of historian and journalist Cornelius Ryan (THE LONGEST DAY, A BRIDGE TOO FAR) wrote from his notes and tapes A PRIVATE BATTLE, the moving documentation of his death from cancer. It is a story of courage and integrity and the magnificent strength of the human spirit. Kathryn has much to say now about the grief process which she believes society is not prepared to deal with. In a recent newspaper interview she stated, "You can mourn two to four weeks. After that you're expected to pick up your life and go on. You're to be terribly strong and not mention the person you lost. In fact," she added, "grief can last three weeks or thirty years."

One thing she is conscious of is her new status, her new role in society. "I can't be Mrs. Cornelius Ryan any more," she said. "I have to be Kathryn Morgan Ryan. When you're no longer a couple, you REALLY are no longer a couple."

Evelyn Murdock echoes this change. "One of the hardest things," she wrote, "was learning to say, 'I, me, mine' instead of 'we, us, our'."

One quietly independent HOM   survivor took the situation in her own hands after the death of her husband. "I couldn't wear my engagement or wedding rings any more. Somehow it didn't seem right. So I had them remade into brand new rings." She looked at her hands and continued. "I'm not just a widow. I'm me - Esther Leatherwood. I can't be tied to a memory. Wherever Don is, he wants me to be somebody on my own. And," she finished with pride, "I am!"

Others wear their widowhood like an impenetrable shield, remaining the visible half of a couple the rest of their lives. Here, as in other situations, people remain true to who and what they are.

FROM THE TIME my five children were small, I've watched with amazement their totally individual responses to crisis. During years of single parenthood, the emotional volcano I lived on often erupted while I struggled to prepare dinner after a day of teaching. At the drop of a spoon, I would go slightly crazy.

When this happened, the children moved quickly into personally delineated roles with such consistency that I, fascinated, forgot my own blow-up watching them.

Chris, the oldest, assumed command and delegated chores (nobody listened). Bruce, next in line, stepped in to continue whatever I'd been doing. Cathi, the only other female, threw a bigger tizzy than I (nobody listened). Steve, however disturbed inside, calmly continued to practice the piano or some such separate activity. And young Jon, crying, "Don't, Mommy, don't be mad!" would seek me out and rub my back. (Ah, that one!). I can almost predict their response to the 'windstorms of life' from this oft-repeated vignette. Even older, each is true to that basic nature.

We are what we are. To change ourselves is a conscious act rather than an automatic happening. It comes from within, a deliberate stretching and reaching, not from external pressures, however overwhelming. The Chinese character for crisis means both danger and opportunity. Certainly the crisis of bereavement carries with it both danger of the unknown and opportunity for growth and change. You can make of it what you choose.

"Jan provided much more of the structure than I did," Ron McCamish, a widower with two young children tells me. "I'd been a very dependent person without knowing it. Suddenly, about a week after the burial, I was alone. Everybody who'd been bringing casseroles and helping with the kids went away." Sounding angry, he continues. "I felt cheated and scared.

"I called the HOM people together, those who'd been so great during Jan's dying. I remember, it was late at night and I was desperate. I demanded they do something. And they - lovingly and stubbornly - told me off! 'You're going to have to work around that,' they said, opening up a whole new thing. They couldn't do it. All was up to me.

"So," he adds, "I went beyond grief to growth. I changed. I'm only sorry Jan can't know me now!"

GRIEF TAKES unusual twists. Dr. Lamers tells of a family where the father was dying. For a long time everyone knew of the impending death and did what they could to support him and each other. When he finally died there was little grief expressed. Sadness, yes, but it was an expected death and they carried on well.

A week later, suddenly, the man's dog died. With this, the entire family fell apart, broke down out of all proportion to the pet's death. They were inconsolable, totally bereaved. Crying tears none had known existed, each was really weeping for the lost husband, father,

brother, uncle, son, not the poor little mutt who triggered their grief.

That reminds me of learning during the final week
of mother's life that the tall wonderful trees lining
most of the streets in our town had contracted Dutch
elm disease and faced destruction. I was driving down
Shady Lane, aptly named, where branches form a
green cathedral dome high overhead. Suddenly I was
crying. "No, no! Not these elms. They're not dying.
Damn it, that I can't bear!" Tears of rage, frustration,
pain, sorrow, loss, came pouring out. I pulled into a
driveway and sat weeping. For the trees?

Tears are strange. Once when I was very young,
mother asked what was wrong. I answered (she often
told me later), "I was crying because I hurt my knee.
Now I'm crying for all the sad and sorry things in the
whole wide world."

That's why weeping, often unexpected, is such a
release. Whether it starts for a dead dog or dying
trees or a scuffed knee, it triggers some hidden switch
and out come tears for all the sad and sorry things in
your entire world.

HOSPICE OF MARIN holds monthly bereavement
gatherings plus occasional bereavement specials. Different in structure and content, each is de-
signed to support bereaved as they work through the
grief process. The gatherings are informal and do
much to remove those feelings of social alienation that
follow a spouse's death, the sense of not belonging in
a group. Here, mutual loss is both a bond and an
ice-breaker. You'll find it easier to talk if you have no
need to explain where you're coming from. (Chances
are the person you're talking to has been there quite
recently!) Some survivors attend one or two meetings; others return month after month, progressing

slowly from tentative guest with a fresh aching loss to become, as many have, voluntary and spontaneous peer counselors. Deep lasting friendships have grown from these gatherings and the support system they provide.

Specials, led by Bill Lamers and Wendy Foster, are more formal and structured. New people show up at each meeting, along with 'regulars,' so an overview of the bereavement process is presented first. Then a general discussion takes place, a sharing that is also a seeking. Dr. Lamers has said many times, "We learn from each other." This is never truer than at such a meeting. Surely as the conversation bounces around the room, insights into the human spirit and its diverse manner of coping are exposed.

HOW LONG does the 'mad' go on?" asks David Ross, a man who overcame his own ill health to attend a dying wife. "I'm not mad at Charlotte. I'm not mad at God. I'm just mad!" He leans forward on his cane. "Sometimes I say to her rocking chair, 'Why are you empty? Charlotte should be sitting there!'"

Jim White nods in understanding. "The injustice still gets to me. That such a beautiful person had to die! What had she ever done?" He shakes his head sadly. "It's been eighteen months since Jenifer's death and I still feel the unfairness."

Aleksandra Glazunova speaks softly with her Russian accent. "To me, every day before he died was full of excitement, beauty. Everything - a leaf, the sun, shadow - filled with vonder. Now, emptiness. The vondermont has gone from the vorld."

"I remember how strange your cat acted right after Sergei's death," says Bill Lamers.

"Yes," agrees Aleksandra, "Smokey's still veird. Vhen she hears a man's voice, she runs toward it. Then she stops and looks so dejected. She sits in the closet a lot. I know how she feels."

"What do you do," asks Bill, "instead of sitting in the closet?"

"I buy coats," she says. "No, really. I go to the store and buy a fantastic coat and bring it home. The next day, back to the store it goes." She plucks at her sleeve. "And I wear this old thing. I keep doing that, buying coats, sending them back."

"Helen," suggests Bill, "share what you did."

"Changed hinges on the kitchen cabinets," Helen Ratto answers with a laugh. "I'd never done anything like that before. It was hard! I'd get all the hinges changed. Then I wouldn't like the way they looked either. So I'd buy some more and do it again."

"You might say," adds Esther Leatherwood, "she became unhinged." We all laugh.

Ken Fahy looks up. "Acceptance of God's plan helped me," he says quietly. "Funny, I never thought much about religion before. But when I could accept Claire's death as part of a bigger plan, that made it easier."

STRANGELY, OR maybe it's not strange at all, many of the responses to Dr. Lamer's question, "What helped in the early days of bereavement?" are the same as those given by other HOM survivors as helpful during the dying of their intimate. For some crying helps, screaming, expressing anger. Others build things, pounding nails with a vengeance (or changing hinges!). Long solitary walks and hard exercise relieve many. Gardening is a welcome outlet as is the difficult involvement with financial and legal details. Friends who could offer clear support and sympathy, doing such heart-rending chores as cleaning out drawers and closets, are invaluable. Unexpected conversations on buses, letters, reaching out to people, giving of yourself, all these are helps. Religion is a mainstay for many. Others agree that to do something crazy and out of character is a boost. Going back to school whether to fill a gap for assuming new roles and responsibilities or merely to learn something challenging, is a possibility utilized by several. Almost all mentioned the wonder of a sense of humor.

And Hospice of Marin! Not one of these vital coping people would be sitting in this room, sharing these insights were it not for an organization such as HOM. It hurts to think of all those bereaved who haven't found such support to put them in touch with their own resources.

DICK AND I have had many discussions during the writing of this book, starting actually in the days of my mother's dying. We have, I feel, come to grips with our own mortality. We know chances are almost 100 percent that one of us will see the other through a terminal illness. One will die first, one face bereavement. Already we both are doing little things that will help the other; learning more about ourselves, our needs and our partner's needs. Talking, always talking, making wills, discussing insurance policies, assets, resources, what the survivor will have to do. Matter-of-factly such things have become part of our conversations.

Planning far ahead, when we added a bedroom to the little cottage in the garden, the bed itself was placed on a higher than normal platform of drawers - easier to get out of and easier to care for someone in. The bathroom is mere steps away. Unless we choose to join the children in the main house for meals, a tiny kitchen serves all our needs. And will later while one of us is dying. Until death and after, this place will accommodate us.

It's comforting to have made these plans and worked through our fears.

R AYMOND MOODY in his book, LIFE AFTER LIFE, and the newer, REFLECTIONS ON LIFE AFTER LIFE, cites many examples of near-death experiences where people mention going through a dark tunnel to reach a place of incredible light and beauty.

Bereavement, I feel, goes through similar darkness, similar constriction, and reaches, in time, a place of light. Your life after an intimate's death will never be the same. But it will be.

T HE END is but another beginning. . .

BIBLIOGRAPHY

Easson, William M. THE DYING CHILD, Springfield, Illinois, Charles
        Thomas, 1970
Freese, Arthur, LIVING THROUGH GRIEF AND GROWING WITH IT, New York
        Barnes & Noble (Harper Row) 1977
Grollman, Earl A. LIVING WHEN A LOVED ONE HAS DIED, Boston, Mass-
        achusetts,Beacon Press, 1977
        TALKING ABOUT DEATH: A Dialogue Between Parent and Child,
        Boston, Beacon Press, 1796
Jackson, Edgar, TELLING A CHILD ABOUT DEATH, New York, Channel
        Press, 1965
        YOU AND YOUR GRIEF, New York, Hawthorn Books, 1962
Jury, Mark and Dan, GRAMPS: A Man Ages and Dies, New York,
        Grossman, 1965
Kastenbaum, Robert, DEATH, SOCIETY AND HUMAN EXPERIENCE, St. Louis
        Missouri, Mosby Press, 1977
Kavanaugh, Robert E. FACING DEATH, Baltimore, Maryland, Penquin
        Books Inc. 1974
LeShan, Eda J. LEARNING TO SAY GOODBYE, New York, MacMillian
        Publishing Co. 1976
Levitt, Rose, ELLEN: A Short Life Long Remembered, San Francisco,
        California, San Francisco Chronicle Books, 1974
Kübler-Ross, Elisabeth, ON DEATH AND DYING, New York, MacMillian
        Publishing Co. Inc. 1969
        DEATH,THE FINAL STAGE OF GROWTH, Englewood Cliffs, New
        Jersey, Hall Inc. 1975
        TO LIVE UNTIL WE SAY GOODBYE, Englewood Cliffs, New Jersey,
        1978
Mitford, Jessica, THE AMERICAN WAY OF DEATH, Greenwich, Connect-
        icut, Fawcett Crest Books, 1963
Moody, Raymond, LIFE AFTER LIFE, New York, Bantam Books Inc. 1975
        REFLECTIONS ON LIFE AFTER LIFE, New York, Bantam Books
        Inc. 1978
Parkes, Colin Murray, BEREAVEMENT: Stages of Grief in Adult Life,
        New York, International Universities Press, 1972
Pine, Vanderlyn R. CARETAKER OF THE DEAD, Halsted Pt. 1979
Roach, Nancy, THE LAST DAY OF APRIL, San Francisco, California,
        American Cancer Society, 1974
Rudolph, Marguerita, SHOULD THE CHILDREN KNOW? New York, Schocken
        Books, 1978
Ryan, Cornelius and Kathryn, A PRIVATE BATTLE, New York, Simon &
        Schuster, 1979
Stein, Sara Bonnett, ABOUT DYING, New York, Walker & Co 1974
Stoddard, Sandol, THE HOSPICE MOVEMENT: A Better Way of Caring
        for the Dying, New York, Stein and Day, 1977
Weisman, Avery, ON DYING AND DENYING, New York, Behavorial
        Publications, 1970

S P E C I A L   A C K N O W L E D G M E N T S

DEATH AND DYING: Challenge and Change, a 15-article series, was developed for COURSES BY NEWSPAPER, through University Extension, University of California, San Diego.

Locally accredited by College of Marin, Kentfield, California, the series appeared in NOVATO ADVANCE, a weekly newspaper published in Novato, California. The series was invaluable to me, opening many avenues. Quotations, used on pages shown, were taken from the following articles:

1. Pages 10, 52: George E. Williams, PREPARE A CHILD TO DEAL WITH DEATH* March 28, 1979. Dr. William is assistant dean of student affairs at the medical school and associate professor of psychiatry at University of Minnesota. He is creator of "Talking to Children about Death," an audio program prepared by the Center for Death Education and Research.

2. Pages 11, 19, 25, 46: Avery D. Weisman, THE DYING PATIENT* March 21, 1979. Dr. Weisman is professor of psychiatry at Massachusetts General Hospital and Harvard Medical School. He is also principal investigator for Project Omega, a research group studying the coping and vulnerability in cancer patients.

3. Page 16: Eric Cassell, DEATH VIEWED AS TECHNOLOGICAL FAILURE* March 7, 1979. Dr. Cassell is clinical professor of public health at Cornell University Medical College, an internist in private practice in New York City.

4. Page 16: Robert Kastenbaum, AMERICAN APPROACH TO DEATH AND DYING NEEDS UPDATING* May 16, 1979. Dr. Kastenbaum is superintendent of Cushing Hospital in Framingham, Massachusetts. He is editor of "International Journal of Aging and Human Development" and of "Omega, Journal of Dying and Death."

5. Pages 40, 47, 49: Colin Murray Parkes, GRIEF: A NATURAL AND NORMAL REACTION WITH A PREDICTABLE PATTERN* April 4, 1979. Dr. Parkes is senior lecturer in psychiatry at London Medical College and consultant psychiatrist to St. Christopher's Hospice, London.

6. Page 43: Vanderlyn R. Pine, FUNERALS FILL A NEED* April 18, 1979. Dr. Pine is associate professor of sociology at State University of New York at New Paltz.

*Copyright ©1979 by the Regents of the University of California. These articles were originally written for the tenth Course by Newspaper "Death and Dying: Challenge and Change." Courses by Newspaper is a project of University Extension, University of California, San Diego, and is funded by the National Endowment for the Humanities.   Reprinted by permission.

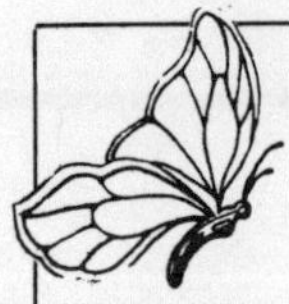

ACKNOWLEDGMENTS

Cindy Brewer for asking questions that started this undertaking.

Hospice of Marin survivors for providing heartfelt answers:
Kathleen "Tut" Anderson, Ken Fahy, Aleksandra Glazunova,
Ruth Goodyear, Jean Guthrie, Margaret Harris, Esther Leather-
wood, Ruth Markt, Ron McCamish, Stephanie Nowell, Helen
Ratto, Gladys Riggs, David Ross, Madeline Trotter, Jim White,
and many others who just by being at the HOM Bereavement
Gatherings made a difference.

Hospice of Marin staff for support all along the way, particularly
Mary Taverna, executive director, and Joanne Hively, public
information director, for their tough editing, and Jean Price for
her enthusiasm.

Busy people for taking time from their crowded schedules to read
and comment on the manuscript: Earl Grollman, Bill Lamers,
Noranel Neely, Howard Raether, Sandol Stoddard and Joy Watts,
to name a few.

Debra Cooper for designing the butterfly reproduced throughout
the book.

Printed by

RAM GRAPHICS
63 Paul Drive,
San Rafael, CA 94903

Copy-work and reductions by

RAM INSTA-PRINT
601 Town & Country Village
Mill Valley, CA 94941

JAYNE MAY MURDOCK, a second generation Californian, was born in San Francisco a month after the end of World War I. Except for time away during college, a war, and marriage to a marine, she has lived at the same family home in Ross, Marin County, since 1924. After graduating from UC Berkeley with a major in journalism in 1940, Jayne spent three years of World War II in the US Marine Corps.

Divorced and needing more daytime hours with her five children during their growing years, she left the newspaper world in 1965 to obtain a teaching credential from Dominican College, San Rafael. Presently a second grade teacher in Mill Valley, she plans to retire by June 1980.

With her third (and last!) husband, Dick Murdock, a retired locomotive engineer, she co-authored LOVE LINES, now in its fourth printing. Jayne edited and did layout on Dick's recent book, HOGHEADS AND HIGHBALLS: Railroad Lore and Humor.

UNTIL DEATH AND AFTER is their sixth collaborative accomplishment, the first, but not the last, in this field. Jayne and her sister, Susan Shepard, an RN, are already preparing the next publication from Susan's experience with dying patients.

The Murdocks are a true literary team doing everything on their respective books except the actual printing. Any of their writings can be ordered from MAY-MURDOCK PUBLICATIONS, Box 343/90 Glenwood Avenue, Ross, CA 94957.